KARMA CREDITS

THE UNIVERSAL LAW OF WEALTH, HEALTH AND HAPPINESS

DANIEL HILL

Rethink

First published in Great Britain in 2022
by Rethink Press (www.rethinkpress.com)

Cover image 'stars' © Klemen Vrankar / Unsplash

Cover image 'coin' © Ingram Image

This book is dedicated to my parents, who showed me
how giving more than you take is the ultimate gift.

Contents

Introduction

Have you ever wondered why some people appear to have it all, why they seem to be so 'lucky'? Have you ever wondered why some people appear to always be down on their luck, faced with problem after problem, and generally aren't having a good time?

If you're seeking to increase your luck, improve connections, enjoy more happiness and experience the rewards of life to the fullest even through periods of challenge, the concept of Karma Credits™ is the secret you have been searching for.[1]

I have committed my life to date to the study and practice of the art of personal development and high performance. As my experience and expertise have developed, they have delivered both the professional results of financial returns and recognition with the personal rewards of enjoyment, connection and contentment.

As you come to understand, practise and master Karma Credits, the universal law of wealth, health and happiness, you will realise how success and failure in life can be far more predictable than you may have previously thought. This book has not been written by a monk, a yogi or a spiritual guide. What I am is an investor, entrepreneur and seeker who's dedicated twenty years to studying and mastering the art of success, and who found the secret to wealth, health and happiness in the most surprising place. Via this book, I am making it immediately accessible to the masses.

INTRODUCTION

Mastering the art of Karma Credits did not move me to live in the mountains nor shift my focus away from being a capitalist investor or entrepreneur in any capacity. What it did was show me how to approach my work and life from a completely different perspective; one that is far more fulfilling, enjoyable, rewarding and predictable, even when times are hard. The moment I realigned my focus towards energy over economics, giving rather than taking and relationships over transactions, my world changed beyond recognition. I have not looked back since.

Initially, the practices in this book may sound or feel awkward and uncomfortable, but if you persevere, I guarantee that the generation and preservation of Karma Credits will become addictive. You'll increase your positive experiences, reduce the negative ones and, from a strong place, be able to handle any challenges that arise.

Whether you choose to use Karma Credits to make your millions in business, improve your mental and physical wellbeing, develop your relationships or find connection, contentment and happiness in this world, the method is the same. The secret to your success is in the pages of this book.

Karma Credits, the universal law of wealth, health and happiness, is the single most powerful attribute that underwrites everything I have, everything I do, everything I have become and everything I pursue. It is far more predictable and achievable than you may think, but until now, it has been poorly defined, grossly misunderstood and, in most cases, mistaught.

I have set out the chapters in this book to follow my ENERGY blueprint:

- Explain
- Noble

- Experience
- Recognise
- Guilt
- Your life

The elements of this model may seem a little random or out of context here, but rest assured: as we work through each one, you will come to understand how to apply Karma Credits, learning how your actions, words and thoughts directly impact your ability to face your life either positively or negatively. This really is a case of reaping what you sow.

I'm not saying that Karma Credits will ensure that only good things will happen to you; none of us can control the world around us, which has a habit of throwing curveballs our way when we least expect them. What I can guarantee is that a positive Karma Credit balance will have untold benefits on you personally: on your mental health, wellbeing, resilience and impact as well as fundamentally changing the world around you and the life you experience daily.

Success and failure are both predictable. Karma Credits is my gift to you. Learn it, practise it, master it – and then pass it on.

Namaste.

ONE
Explain

Karma [kahr-muh] Noun: Hinduism, Buddhism.
Action, seen as bringing upon oneself inevitable
results, good or bad, either in this life or in a
reincarnation[2]

In Buddhism, karma is understood as the natural law of cause and effect. According to Venerable Mahasi Sayadaw in 'The theory of karma in Buddhism', the 'sequence of deed and effect is as natural and necessary as the way of the sun and the moon'.[3] As each of our actions creates an energy, it stands to reason that a reciprocal reaction returns to us.

Put simply, when you create and put out positive energy, good things will come back to you. When you create and put out negative energy, bad things will come back to you. The karma you experience in your everyday life is, therefore, a direct reflection of everything you choose to say, think and do on a daily basis.

I devised and developed the concept of Karma Credits to enable me to share with you the message and practice that have served me so well. The term Karma Credits is original; I coined it to define the universal currency that governs how the law of wealth, health and happiness is distributed. Although these credits cannot be explicitly measured or calibrated, the self-awareness you will gain through the practice of Karma Credits provides a consciously measured balance. In other words, the way you experience the world, in both good times and bad, will change.

As you work through the ENERGY model, you will learn and come to understand how to master and control both the tangible and intangible effects of karma in and around your everyday life. Often, people regard the energy created by karma and the subsequent actions they experience from it as a somewhat invisible force of nature, but by using Karma Credits, you will quickly experience the real impact this has on your life.

Universal law of justice

As a universal law of justice, Karma Credits is a credit-based system to recognise and reflect everything you think, say and do, both in public and in private. This reflection is based on the positive and negative energy these actions create, delivering a comparable reaction in return.

When you think, say or do something positive, you will generate Karma Credits to reflect the significance of that good action. These credits increase your balance and are reflected in either the positive reaction you will experience in return or the strength, energy and confidence you gain to face a challenge when it presents itself.

When you think, say or do something negative, you will lose an amount of Karma Credits to reflect the significance of that bad action. This reduces your balance and is reflected by either the negative reaction you will experience in return or a weakening in your ability to overcome challenges when they arise.

Essentially, if you are a genuinely good person who, consciously and subconsciously, does, says and thinks wholesome, helpful, positive and pleasant things, you will generate good energy. This will be reflected in the quality of life you experience as positive karma supports you on your journey. The same applies in the negative.

External action and internal impact

The daily increase or decrease of your Karma Credits balance is an external action which has an internal impact. Not only do your outward actions define how you experience the external world, but the reaction from them defines the energy and feeling of the internal world that you create and experience.

The generation or loss of Karma Credits by saying or doing good or bad things may seem like a primarily external action, but do not underestimate the internal impact karma has on who you are fundamentally and how you ultimately feel. As you master the external art of generating and retaining Karma Credits in your life, many of the most significant benefits you will experience will be internal. You will develop an increasing feeling of contentment that builds your confidence, establishes your connections, and generates a rich and rewarding experience and enjoyment in your life despite the challenges your journey may present you with.

In the broadest sense, if you go about your day being selfless and adding value to others, this will generate Karma Credits that will manifest as positive energy and good actions in your life in the days, weeks and months ahead. Being selfless is about putting the needs and wants of others ahead of your own, giving more than you take and doing so from a place of authentic, genuine care.

Selflessness enables you to generate Karma Credits that protect you on your way. As you act from the heart and the soul rather than the ego, you will start your journey of connection with those around you and develop more genuine and meaningful relationships.

Selfishness is the opposite. At face value, being selfish may present you with a seductive appeal of self-service, instant gratification and looking after number one, but in most cases, this approach is a short-sighted perspective. It holds limited to no value or returns in the medium to long term.

If you go about your day behaving selfishly with the primary objective of getting everything you can and doing only what you want while discarding the interests, perspectives, objectives, requirements, opinions and experiences of others, the upset you cause will create negative energy. This in turn will cost you Karma Credits and reduce your balance. You may not consciously appreciate or experience the consequences of these actions immediately, but in the medium and long term, the impact will be significant and, when you look back, in most cases explicitly obvious.

When you understand how to generate Karma Credits and improve the quality, experience and results you achieve in your life, you will see that the mindsets, mantras and attitudes driven by mass society, particularly in the western world, appear to be conspiring against this way of life. This is why the practice I will describe in this book may at first seem odd or awkward, but you will soon appreciate the benefits. The likelihood then is that you will feel compelled to practise this in every moment of your day and increasingly struggle to understand why others are not doing the same.

Initially, as you develop self-awareness by acknowledging any negative thoughts, attitudes and actions you have or take daily, you will begin to appreciate the effect these have on a situation or encounter both as it happens and in the medium to long term. The next step is to reconsider your approach proactively and consciously in these scenarios and, in many cases, revise your attitude and actions.

EVERY ACTION HAS A CONSEQUENCE

Having studied and practised Karma Credits, I now have the understanding and experience to review in hindsight both the positive and negative experiences I have had. How I was able to attract and/or manage those experiences has made it clear that success or failure in each case was predictable.

As soon as the concept that every action I took would lead to a reaction resonated with me, I became obsessed with reviewing and revising my thoughts, actions and behaviours. Originally, to gain confidence in this practice, I had to deal with the basics like biting my tongue rather than speaking my mind or pushing myself out of my comfort zone to deliver a selfless act to a stranger. Not only did this practice offer some nice quick wins, but now it is so well established in me, I am at the point where I cannot walk past a stranger without smiling and saying hello, cannot hear a sneeze in public without saying 'bless you' or am unable to rush over to pick up a dropped item the second I spot one.

In reflecting on the actions and reactions of my personal and professional life, I have critiqued key events and relationships that have made me, as well as the wrong turns and moments of madness that could have broken me.

In my younger days, when I behaved in a relationship in a way I would now judge as unfavourable, karma came back around and, ultimately, I was the one who ended up losing out.

Equally, in business when I have been faced with the choice of either looking after number one and taking what I can in the moment or taking a hit today and playing the long game for tomorrow, every time I have taken the latter, the rewards have been returned tenfold.

What is evident is that the investment I have made in choosing to do good actions and generate a positive Karma Credits balance is the number-one factor that has got me to where I am. Even when the ongoing challenges of business and life present themselves, these actions and the subsequent Karma Credits insurance policy they provide give me an underlying feeling of contentment and confidence, and they appear to somehow protect me when required and keep me in a good place.

TWO
Noble

Noble /ˈnəʊb(ə)l/ Adjective: Having or showing fine personal qualities or high moral principles[4]

In its simplest form, being noble is about asking yourself each day, 'How can I best serve here?' and 'What can I do today to add value to those around me?'

I'm neither a socialist nor a charity. I run commercially driven enterprises that deliver net financial gains, but my mindset, approach and motivation are all driven by the notion of how much value I can add to every stakeholder involved.

Fine personal qualities

To introduce a sense and state of nobility into your life, you will need to appraise, identify and choose the fine personal qualities you would like to live by – those which you would like to define you. To do this, take some time to consider:

- Who you are and who you want to be
- What core personal values and traits you find endearing in others and would like to cultivate within yourself
- What you need to do to enable you to be proud of yourself

While society would define me as a high-achieving entrepreneur who has attained many of the accolades and rewards associated with professional success, I pride myself on being humble, approachable and understated. I live an unassuming and modest lifestyle in the main as these are the fine personal qualities and core values that are important to me.

Professionally, I pride myself on the fine personal quality of being able to 'lead from the back' by identifying high-potential individuals to invest my time, effort and energy in. Within a framework of explicit clarity and shared understanding that is congruent with the definition I hold of my noble self and the associated fine personal qualities, I put my objectives and interests behind those of my team, investors, clients and stakeholders to focus primarily on how I can best serve each of them. In the long term, this will serve me as much as it serves them; the win-win outcome provides everyone involved with what they are looking for.

When I meet someone for the first time, I frequently receive feedback that I am nothing like the person they were expecting me to be. Perhaps it's because stereotypically, society perceives high-achievers and those of financial means to be arrogant, unrelatable and pretentious, so people are genuinely surprised when I turn up wearing the same £5 black T-shirt and non-branded jeans every time, and openly exhibit many of the same life challenges, faults and flaws as everyone else.

These are the fine qualities that I have selected for myself and developed over the years, and which I now pride myself on. Yours may be different, so I encourage you to dig deep to identify what qualities you have and/or would like to be associated with as you begin this next phase of your life.

Once you've developed and established your state of nobility, you will achieve a level of peace, confidence and contentment, and a sense of being that is lacking in today's culture and society. Via this practice, you can enjoy a way of life that at present is gifted to the rare few.

High moral values

Along with the fine personal qualities that lay the foundations of nobility, you will need to explore, define, understand and exercise your own set of high moral values. This is the secret to generating and retaining Karma Credits. Despite what the short-term implications and impact might be of you putting these into place, you must abide by them regardless.

Many people, especially in work and business, focus their mindset and attention on the transaction at hand. They live their lives based on what they can gain from a real-time interaction going on today rather than taking a broader and longer-term view. If you are to rise above the masses to a high level of value, attraction and abundance, you need to explore, understand and select which moral values will serve you best. Move away from the default narcissistic mindset of capitalising on every transaction to get what you want in the moment to one of developing high value and meaningful relationships. This may require a concession today but will deliver maximum enjoyment and return for tomorrow.

One of my key moral values is to do the right thing, regardless of the short-term impact or cost this can have. This could mean losing a deal or suffering a financial loss, but if it's the right thing to do, I must do it. The positive Karma Credits I generate from doing so will play out in my favour in the long run.

When you live your life by your high moral values and grasp concepts like doing the right thing and moving to a mindset of relationships over transactions, you will align your objectives and actions with the big picture. This will help you to keep doing the right thing, even when you're confronted with a situation that seems to force you to behave without integrity. When you need to step up and take the hit, make sure you do so. Karma Credits are all about playing the long game, which as you will be aware, is far easier said than done.

Adding value

A fundamental mindset within the law of karma and the generation of Karma Credits is to have an exclusive and selfless attitude with a complete focus on adding value to everyone around you. It doesn't matter what personal development, economic, business, religious or spiritual text you read, the core fundamental of all high-value relationships and exchanges in life is to be of service, so focus on how much you can give rather than how much you can take.

Giving is living. Once you decide to move your primary focus in this direction, not only will you meet less resistance and your experiences feel more rewarding, but your returns and credits will accumulate and quickly compound.

Most people go through life with a mindset of scarcity. It's every person for themselves, their cards held close to their chest, feeling that everyone is out to get them. As a result, they are out to grab everything they can.

At the most basic level, consciously switch your thinking away from a mindset of fear and scarcity to one of abundance and connection. Then you will see and experience the limitless potential in life. In this world, there is more than enough to go around, and the more you give, the more you will end up receiving.

As you develop this mindset, you will see and feel the abundance of potential in yourself and everyone around you. Your new default motivation will focus on adding value to everyone you encounter, enabling your positive energy to flow freely and effortlessly as you progress to a level of enjoyment and nobility that the masses would never even consider.

How can you, right now, start being noble and add value to someone else's day? How can you move from a mindset of scarcity, where it's everyone for themselves, to one of abundance, where we're all in this together?

Simply ask every person you meet from today onwards how their day is going. When you get on the bus, ask the driver, 'How's your day going?' When you're at the supermarket, ask the cashier, 'How are you? Are you having a good day today?' Implement this and it will change your life forever.

What this tiny but high-value gesture does is add value to the other person and replaces a traditionally functional transaction with a warm and human connection. By breaking the potential monotony or stress of a person's challenging day with a genuinely caring enquiry, you can lift their spirits and bring a smile to their face.

This practice is not a wholly selfless exercise. It will support your transition towards an abundance mindset, break down the perception you may have of engaging with strangers being potentially intimidating and build the confidence, energy and connection you have with the world around you.

How is your day going today? Start using this simple but life-changing one-liner with everyone you encounter. Your eyes will then open to the vast array of opportunities that exists outside of the fast-paced mobile-phone life and personal agendas of the modern world as your engagement and enjoyment levels increase significantly.

Daily actions

Here are some quick wins: easy ways for you to be noble, serve others, add value and get the feel-good factor to generate those all-important Karma Credits as you go about your day:

- Open/hold the door for people and be the last one to walk through it. Leaders walk through the door last.

- Let people out in traffic. How many times have you waited at a T-junction and not a single soul has let you out? Be kind. As long as it's safe to do so, let someone out at a junction or merge lanes in front of you in traffic.

- Pick things up for people. Grab any opportunity to spend thirty seconds lending a helping hand and you will make that person's day.

- Make eye contact, say hello and smile at everyone who crosses your path today.

Never underestimate how much value it can add to someone's day to be greeted warmly, noticed and validated.

- Save a life. I go out of my way to save any living creature, no matter how small, as I just can't watch something die. Jain monks carry a *picchi*, a broom made up of fallen peacock feathers, to move small insects from their path as they walk. Save an insect today and start your journey connecting with one and all around you.

While these are seemingly small actions, they convert into real Karma Credits that will accumulate into life-changing experiences and results. Life is all for one, not one-on-one. When you understand and appreciate that you are part of something much bigger than yourself, you'll realise that you have a lot more control over this world and life than you may currently think.

BE SOMEONE YOU CAN BE PROUD OF

This anecdote is a significant moment for me, which has remained untold in the main until now (for reasons we will explore later in this book).

Several years ago, I was waiting at a red light when the driver behind me drove into my car. Instead of getting upset, I remained calm and decided to make a positive connection and do the right thing to resolve this situation without issue.

I got out of the car to speak to the driver and enquired if he was OK. He said he was fine and apologised profusely, but he was visibly upset, nervous and anxious. I tried to reassure him by saying it was not a problem, suggesting we pull into the layby ahead and swap details.

Safely parked in the layby, we continued our conversation. The other driver was still visibly shaking as he got out of the car and walked towards me. Tearful and distressed, he told me how sorry he was for hitting my car and that, despite it still being mid-morning, he was having the worst day. He explained his mum was ill in hospital, that he'd sat with her throughout the night, but he'd had to leave her that morning as he needed to work. He was a taxi driver, and on his first job that morning, the person he'd picked up had fled without paying. On his way to his second job, he had bumped into my car.

I couldn't see any obvious damage to either car, so we exchanged details. Assuring him that I wouldn't make a claim, I asked him how much the unpaid fare was. It was £12.50.

I walked back to my car, took out a £20 note and handed it to the chap. I wasn't worried about my car, so nor should he be. I just hoped the £20 would compensate him for the bad start to his day.

The next day, I received a text message from the driver, saying that he had relayed the story of our encounter to his mother. He told me they had said a prayer for me that night as they were so touched that I had cared.

He said, 'God is looking over you. You are a good man and good things will come to you.'

The perfect ending to this story would be, of course, for me to have regained the £20 I handed over in some unexpected way, but the consequences of acting from a place of fine personal qualities and high moral values are often a lot less tangible. You never know which act will deliver a return, or when that will take place, but that is not the point. That day brought with it challenges for me, both personal and professional, some of which had the potential to be extremely stressful. With the contentment, confidence and Karma Credits generated by my small act of kindness, I was able to approach each one of them with a smile on my face and a mindset positively brimming with abundance.

This encounter with the taxi driver touched me and still does a decade later, but back then, what I did was just the right thing to do. It is an approach I have taken many times since, and I would encourage you to do the same.

Be a good person. Be noble. Be someone you can be proud of.

THREE
Experience

Experience /ɪkˈspɪərɪəns, ɛkˈspɪərɪəns/ Noun: An event or occurrence which leaves an impression on someone[5]

Life is an experience. I invite you to consider the notion that you have far more control over how your experience of life plays out than you may think.

This approach applies whether you're in a good place or a bad place. Where you are and how you feel today is the result of yesterday's thoughts and actions – and it's cyclical. When things are going great, it is only a matter of time until you inevitably encounter challenges. Equally, when things are really challenging, things will invariably go full circle and once again come good.

Whether you believe your experience of life is completely in your control or that you have no control at all, positive Karma Credits increase the volume of good and enjoyable exchanges you encounter and decrease the negative ones, as well as making those you do face easier to overcome. This chapter explores the actions, attitudes and gestures you can proactively take daily to generate these positive Karma Credits and increase the level of enjoyment and fulfilment you get from each day.

The impression that you leave when you act with nobility delivers a feel-good factor for all involved. You feel the positive energy internally and see it extended externally to others.

At that moment in time, you change the world around you and your experience within it. You are creating positive actions that subsequently return positive reactions that you will literally see, experience and feel.

There is scientific proof that the human brain, one of the most advanced and complex creations on the planet, has a high level of plasticity, meaning it can be easily influenced, trained, controlled or intentionally developed.[6] The environment and energy around you is the same in that it is highly malleable and can be significantly adjusted, impacted and improved by a consistent application of positive vibrations.

If your academic or logical mind is questioning how you can 'see' positive vibrations or 'feel' positive energy in practice, here is an example of a scenario with which you can experiment. Next time you are around a negative person (often called a 'drain') or a positive person (a 'radiator'), tune into your self-awareness and watch the energy either drain from the room or radiate into it. Feel the impact this has on the environment that everyone around the drain or radiator is experiencing. Once your eyes have opened, the early layers of your energy awareness will have been established.

These are big topics and bold statements, but if you are to break away from the masses and enjoy your experience of life to the fullest, it's time to understand the basics. Try this experiment for yourself and see the positive (or negative) vibrations play out.

Random acts of kindness (RAKs)

A RAK is a selfless and spontaneous action that you choose to make daily. It's a genuine kindness towards the outside world that bids to add value to others.

Due to the default construct of many modern cultures and societies (arguably more so in the western world), performing a RAK is likely to feel uncomfortable, but once you overcome this and break through the initial discomfort, your confidence will grow. The immediate rewards you will experience in terms of the boost in your own wellbeing will increase your motivation to continue until ultimately, you become addicted and unable to let an opportunity for a RAK pass you by without you acting on it.

Here are some examples of highly valuable RAKs:

- Smile at a stranger
- Say 'Bless you' when someone sneezes
- Give genuine compliments
- Give small gifts of appreciation
- Anonymously pay for a stranger's coffee
- Support someone in their moment of need

- Show gratitude with a thank-you card or public recognition
- Do an act of service for someone else
- Notice and comment on the positive actions of others

A key point to note is that while you can rightly offer a RAK to your existing network of friends, family and co-workers, as soon as your confidence is boosted and a situation presents itself, take this to the next level by imparting these acts to strangers. It will fundamentally improve your daily life experience.

While your interest in Karma Credits and the law of attracting wealth, health and happiness might have a private objective, it is important to understand and recognise that the practice of generating Karma Credits and how these are redeemed sits entirely on the notion of self-lessness. Ultimately, you need to have little or no concern for yourself as you put the needs of others before your own. Later in this book, we will explore the unquestionable power and returns of reciprocity, but before we can even consider that, you must fully understand the selfless approach required to arrive there.

In going about your day intending to give rather than get, seeking where you can be of service and add value to the experience of others, you will tap into the deep and true feelings that are often masked by the masses and the material world. Reordering your objectives in the pursuit of a high level of connection and satisfaction within your experiences involves a mental and practical discipline of going out of your way to help others with no focus on value for yourself, no hidden obligation and no preconceived expectation.

As you test the practice of becoming noble and creating positive vibrations, you will need to look for prompts as to where and when to deliver your first RAK. There are two main formats to consider:

- **A personal RAK.** These are RAKs you perform for someone in person, ie you are both present and you engage with them to deliver or give the RAK to them physically. You are both likely to enjoy the shared experience.

- **A private RAK.** Your RAK is delivered or gifted in private and the person who benefits from it may never know who you are. You may not even see the beneficiary enjoy your RAK, but you will have the reward of knowing that you've selflessly done something good and made someone smile.

Whether your RAK is personal or private, always do it discreetly. There is no value in these actions if shortly after you've undertaken one, you broadcast what you've done to the world via social media to show how amazing you are and seek congratulations or recognition.

This advice may seem contrary to the fact that I have taken the opportunity to share several examples in this book, but this is simply to illustrate RAKs in practice. On the whole, whether you deliver daily RAKs in person or in private, you must keep what you've done to yourself to build you Karma Credits.

It doesn't take much to make a positive impact; it is far more about the sentiment behind the gesture than its size. Here are a few examples of RAKs you can perform while out and about:

- On a train/plane, when the drinks trolley comes past, order yourself a drink and offer to buy one for the person sitting next to you.

- If you see a massage chair at a hotel or an airport, get some change, write a little note saying, 'Have a massage on me' and leave the cash on top of the note.

- If you're somewhere that charges an entry fee to use the public toilets, change a £1 coin for five 20p pieces, use one for yourself and leave the other four at the barriers so the next handful of people can go through for free.

As you go about your day today, seek your first opportunity to perform a RAK, however small. Experience how good it feels to give without expectation, generating positive energy around you and boosting the Karma Credits that will return the favour tenfold when you most need it and probably least expect it.

THE SUPERMARKET CHECKOUT

A great friend of mine, James, shared a perfect example of a RAK. This highlights both how Karma Credits can be generated and how every action leads to a reaction.

James raced up to his local supermarket fifteen minutes before it closed. He grabbed what he needed and queued at the checkout. In front

EXPERIENCE

of him, a guy was checking his pockets, only to
realise he'd left his wallet at home.

With a loaded trolley, the guy was obviously
a family man and was very embarrassed. The
checkout person wanted to go home, the store
was closing and the general vibe was that
everyone wanted out of there.

James saw someone in trouble and without
hesitation stepped in. 'Allow me to cover this
for you,' he said. 'I'll give you my number and
you can sort it out later; it's no trouble.'

The guy's bill was around £240 so he protested
and was still embarrassed, but James let him
know that he'd just been paid and not to worry
about it. Finally, the guy accepted the offer and
they exchanged numbers.

James had simply seen this as an opportunity
to put some positive vibrations and energy
out into the world. In doing so, he felt good
in himself. He had supported the guy without
the wallet, adding value to those waiting in
the queue and the cashier. The cashier even
remarked on how it was the one kind gesture
they'd seen in a day of serving rude and
oblivious characters. Despite causing a minor

delay to them finishing, James's action had put a smile on their face too.

Unsurprisingly, it was not long before James's Karma Credits RAK came full circle. The guy James had helped not only repaid the money he owed, but also approached James with a proposition. He and his wife were thinking about going into property and they'd found via Facebook that James was involved in this industry. They asked James if he would assist them in a paid mentoring capacity as they wanted to repay him further in the future. James was amazed that it had only taken twelve hours for the Karma Credits his RAK had generated to work their magic.

James felt, however, that he had already won. He was ahead in the transaction as he was still energised by the feeling of doing the right thing, so he explained there was zero debt and that if the couple really wanted to pay something back, then all they had to do was look out for the next person they encountered who needed a helping hand and pass the goodwill on.

The gesture of a RAK may be big or small, but it will always create a positive return. When you put positive vibes out there, it supports those around you and leaves a positive impression. I encourage you to try RAKs for yourself. They are great ways to generate Karma Credits. Take action and give it a go today.

FOUR

Recognise

*Recognise /ˈrek.əg.naɪz/ Verb: To show private
and public appreciation for the achievement or
contribution of a person or a group*[7]

In this modern fast-paced world, many of us
drift around on autopilot. We may encounter hundreds of people each day but fail to
connect with any of them due to the distrac-
tion of our phones, preoccupation with our
own agendas or even a general lack of interest
or appreciation.

Taking time to recognise the daily contribution and presence of those around you will bring fresh enjoyment to your day and re-establish your connection to the outside world and those you share it with. Simultaneously, as you observe the masses and do the opposite, it will make you stand out and become someone worth remembering.

The gift of giving

Giving does not necessarily mean a tangible gift, as with many RAKs. It's also how you recognise someone's presence, contribution, service or efforts and show your appreciation for this.

If you take a moment to give the gift of acknowledgement, you will literally change the world around you. Ask people, 'How is your day going?' or offer a simple thank you to recognise someone's contribution in passing.

As you gather momentum, experience and confidence in this practice, you will realise that it is no longer an option and instead becomes something you feel you both want and feel compelled to do.

Entrepreneur and motivational speaker Jim Rohn says, 'One of the greatest gifts you can give to anyone is the gift of your attention.'[8] When you take action to recognise the efforts of others with your attention and appreciation, be it publicly or privately, they feel valued and appreciated. This is one key way in which you establish positive energy, vibrations and connections.

Be it to a stranger or someone with whom you are familiar, gift a 'one-minute moment', where you stop and take some time to say, 'Thank you for doing that. You did a great job,' or, 'Thank you for standing in for me; I really appreciate it,' or, 'Thank you for pre-paring this. You helped me out of a tight spot this morning.' It is extremely important and valuable to say thank you and show gratitude, particularly when people least expect it.

A client of mine took this on board. At the end of a large property refurbishment project, he took the time to send the project manager a private voice message with a genuine thank you for his efforts and let him know that it had been an absolute privilege to work with him. The project manager was completely moved by this unexpected message as it was not something he would usually receive.

In the past in business, at the end of a project, it was my standard procedure to issue the final invoice. The client paid and that was the close of the transaction. Now, once the final invoice is paid, my team and I send a hamper to thank the client for being great to work with. They never expect this and it's a far more engaging way to finalise the contract than just taking their money, closing the door and moving on.

It's the same when I am the client. For example, when I paid an invoice for a world-class supplier, I added 10% to recognise that they had gone above and beyond to deliver a phenomenal job. I coupled this with a personal message, sharing how much I had appreciated their support and that I hoped we could have a long working relationship. The supplier said he couldn't believe it; that in forty years of doing business, no one had ever given him a bonus or a tip. I found that shocking. Because I hadn't followed the masses and had instead recognised the efforts of this supplier, I'm sure it encouraged him to continue his great service and added value to our longstanding relationship.

Small things make the biggest difference

Taking time to show your appreciation and share your thanks does not need to involve grandiose gestures or financial remuneration. While there is a time and a place for this, the smallest things can make the biggest difference.

In my early years of business, every Easter and Christmas, I sent cakes to clients and suppliers. A decade on, I have many significant partners who I genuinely believe I'm still in business with today because of these small gestures of goodwill.

If one of my team members is either celebrating a success or suffering from a loss, I send a handwritten card with a sincere message or a bunch of flowers. This acknowledgement that I know and care goes a long way. On one occasion, a team member contacted me and asked if they could buy one of the spare chairs I had in storage for their son's new desk. I offered up my padded racing chair as I knew their son was into Formula One and would get more enjoyment out of it than I did. They were chuffed with this gift that was given with no expectation of payment or reciprocity, but I was instantly rewarded with great joy as I learned their son had been saving for a chair just like it and it had made him so happy.

It is important here to realise that it is not the size but the sincerity of the recognition you give that counts. If you get into the habit of asking, 'How can I best recognise and add value to those around me?' you'll soon realise that the feeling of giving is one of the best gifts you can receive.

Recognition without expectation

The daily act of seeking to recognise everyone who adds value to your life is only of true benefit if you do it without expectation. I talk about the inevitable return that Karma Credits deliver, but you will only achieve this when you have genuinely earned it. You must approach the practice of giving thanks and showing gratitude from the selfless stance of wishing to recognise others without any expectation of reciprocity. In turn, this will make you someone worth remembering.

Acknowledge everyone who serves you or adds value to your daily life. You can do this for anyone with whom you have a relationship, be it your family, friends or team. As with RAKs, once you have initiated the basic process of acknowledging what those close to home do for you, move further afield and acknowledge all the strangers who serve you in shops, venues and restaurants, or simply those who hold the door open for you.

Seek every opportunity to turn your recognition into action. With no expectation to receive anything in return, actively recognise people's contribution or service appropriately. Friends and family will be easy, but you may have to push yourself out of your comfort zone to take a genuine interest in engaging with those you would otherwise pass without a thought. Engaging with strangers may initially seem odd and awkward, but once you sense the significant positive impact, energy and feeling it creates for you and those around you, it will turn into an addiction that you would not want to proceed through life without.

The law of reciprocity

While it is essential that the objective of recognising others must be unconditional and selfless giving without any expectation of return, you will discover that the law of reciprocity swings into motion as a result. With the Karma Credits you generate, you will begin to experience significant rewards in return.

There's a natural law of reciprocity in every society.[9] This states that when you do a favour for someone, they feel compelled to respond with something equally generous. For example, if someone stops to help you carry a heavy load, it is likely you will then feel indebted to them and want to pay them back in some capacity. In the simplest of forms, as you give the gift of recognition by engaging with strangers, offering thanks and helping others, you will find that the law of reciprocity plays out. As you generate your Karma Credits, your daily interactions become richer and your positive energy increases.

'Be the change you wish to see' is a quote often attributed to Mahatma Gandhi. Whether or not he really said this, it is worth consideration. Have you ever considered in depth what it means? Over the years, as I have incorporated the practice of generating Karma Credits into everything I do, and I have come to appreciate how malleable the world around us and our interactions within it are. Being the change is actively engaging in the practice of performing these acts that generate Karma Credits, to experience and see these returned to you tenfold via the law of reciprocity. Positive karma and energy will come to you in both good times and bad, often when you least expect it or most need it.

A DAY IN THE LIFE OF KARMA CREDITS

To illustrate this, here is a 'day in the life' style overview of Karma Credits in action. This details a day in real time that I experienced while I was writing this book for you.

At my hotel check-in this morning, I engage with the lady who welcomes me, ask her how her day is going and have five minutes of conversation while she prepares the formalities. The six people ahead of me have chosen to play on their phones or chat to their partner rather than engaging with her.

As I walk along the corridor to check into my room, I take a moment to say hello to the

cleaner I pass and wish them a great day.
When I arrive at my room, the key card fails
to work, but the cleaner notices the issue
and immediately comes to my aid, using their
master key to let me in. Coincidence? I suspect
not.

Back downstairs, I enter the hotel bar and a
waiter informs me that it won't be open for
another ninety minutes. I thank him for letting
me know and ask him how his week has been,
then we have a five-minute conversation about
his university degree. I place my order for a
green tea and jug of water ahead of the bar
opening, wish him the best for his day and open
my laptop.

Five minutes later, he returns with my drinks,
saying I can settle the bill when the bar opens.
Standard service everyone gets ninety minutes
before opening time? I suspect not.

After a morning of writing, I have a massage
booked in. Before the treatment commences,
I take a moment to say hello to the therapist
and ask how her day is going. I learn she is
from Thailand and a Buddhist, so I mention
Karma Credits. During the forty-five-minute

RECOGNISE

treatment, she goes on to share all sorts of
advice, insight and wisdom, much of which is
included in this book.

Upon completion of my treatment, she delays
her next client by ten minutes and insists she
walk me to a traditional local Thai restaurant.
Once we are there, she introduces me to the
chef and requests they make me a dish that is
not on the menu. The usual treatment for all
customers? I suspect not.

Returning to the hotel, I approach the now
queue-free reception to get my key card fixed.
The same lady who checked me in is still there,
so I continue our conversation and ask how her
afternoon has been before letting her know my
key card isn't working.

'You're room 626, is that correct?' she asks,
despite having checked in hundreds of people
that day. Does she remember all their room
numbers or just that of the guy who took a
moment to say hi?

Later, out at dinner, I pick up a hat that has
fallen from a chair at the table next to mine
and return it to its owner, who responds with

61

a slightly surprised but genuinely grateful thank you. Having eaten, I am on my way out when the same person initiates a conversation. It transpires that we are in the same line of business in the same city, so I make a new connection just by picking up a hat.

Back at the hotel bar, I decide to get in a couple of hours' writing. The waiter from this morning has returned and says hello, so we continue our conversation and chat about how his university seminar went between his shifts. Shortly afterwards, a pot of green tea and a jug of ice water are delivered to my table, which I gratefully acknowledge and thank him for.

'Would you prefer cash or card?' I ask.

'No payment required, sir,' he replies. 'These are on me.'

This is Karma Credits in action. What a day.

Increase your self-awareness; give without expectation; be someone worth remembering. Recognise the value the people around you bring to your day, and as a result, bring value to their day in return. Take the time to develop the basic practices I describe in this book, and this is how every day will look. As you change, the world around you does likewise.

FIVE
Guilt

Guilt /gilt/ Noun: The fact or state of having committed an offence, crime, violation, or wrong, especially against moral or penal law; culpability[10]

The feeling of guilt is negative and unpleasant. Whether it stems from letting yourself or someone else down, the uncomfortable feeling you carry with you as a result is a classic example of the negative energy you want to avoid.

Guilt, and the negative energy it attracts, will weigh you down and can have repercussions on your life, emotions and mental and physical health. The mantra I encourage you to take forward from this chapter is 'Don't leave crumbs'. Making mistakes – dropping crumbs – is part of life. If you leave these crumbs behind and your issues remain unresolved, be it through ignorance, arrogance or fear, it will attract negative energy into your life.

No one is perfect. I have made terrible mistakes and behaved poorly. I've let myself and others down, so I am more than familiar with the feeling of guilt and the negative energy this attracts. You will never be able to eliminate mistakes from your life completely, nor the associated experience of guilt, but when you take the correct actions to resolve a situation and pick up the dropped 'crumb' promptly, you can certainly minimise the negative impact.

In fact, making mistakes should be encouraged. The more mistakes you make, the faster you learn, progress and grow.

That said, to generate Karma Credits and add value, you want your mistakes to deliver a net positive result for all involved. To do this, you need to develop a level of self-awareness which enables you to recognise the feeling of guilt, acknowledge your misguided decisions and take responsibility for them and your subsequent actions. Mistakes do not define you, but the way that you behave in resolving them does.

When you make mistakes and drop crumbs, do you use the feelings of discomfort and guilt as a learning opportunity? Can the mistake be quickly resolved? Can the resolution be of value to all involved? Through a mindset of denial, ego or arrogance, or a disregard for your own actions, do you leave a situation untended? Does this cause pain, discomfort and potentially permanent scarring for all involved? If you're honest with yourself, you're likely to find it does.

If leaving a problem to fester sounds more akin to your current approach, consider the alternative. Think about what crumbs you've left behind you and how you can go back to do the right thing and clear them up today. Then you can develop the self-awareness and confidence to act accordingly. You are not who you were yesterday.

Negative energy

We are all human and likely to have done things in our lives that we regret – taken a wrong turn; made bad decisions; unintentionally or otherwise upset people. Consequently, we may suffer from a sense of guilt, but how does this manifest as negative energy?

Consider this scenario: you make a poorly considered short-term-focused business decision with somebody who lives in London. This goes wrong and, consequently, you cut all lines of communication with your former business partner. It seems like a logical quick fix to prevent you from experiencing any further discomfort, but this unresolved dispute, this 'crumb', will leave you with negative tension. Each time you visit London, you will likely be looking over your shoulder, wondering if you are going to cross paths with this person. What if your new business contacts in London know this individual? Your dropped crumb could now impact your relationship with them.

This negative energy will become a real burden and adversely affect your experience in life. How others perceive you and your actions coupled with your own self-critique can prevent you from becoming someone you can be genuinely proud of.

If you promise to do something but don't deliver, you are likely to judge yourself unfavourably, attract negative energy into your life and potentially cause damage to your mental wellbeing. You must either stop making promises and then letting yourself down or, if it is something important to you, increase your levels of discipline and self-respect and just get it done.

Deciding to commit to something and then executing on your promise feels great. It will not attract negative energy. Deciding not to commit to something as it's not important enough to you will also not attract negative energy. Saying you are going to do things and then not executing on them will compromise the value of your word, reduce the level of trust and confidence you have in yourself and attract negative energy, which you may or may not be conscious of.

Mistakes that result in the dropping of crumbs tend to be definite events or experiences that you can identify easily. In addition to looking at the actions you take to resolve this crumb dropping, you have an opportunity to take this to a higher level by also analysing your thoughts related to it.

Self-help author and lecturer Bob Proctor eloquently explains that the things that come into your life are 'attracted to you by virtue of the images you're holding in your mind. It's what you're thinking.'[11] The concept of visualisation, affirmation and the law of attraction has been popularised in *The Secret* by Rhonda Byrne,[12] which explores the impact your seemingly intangible thoughts have on your actions, experiences, results and life. I have experienced this in practice. The thoughts I have chosen to concentrate my efforts on, be they positive or negative, have manifested themselves into a reality. The positive ones have fundamentally forged my journey of wealth, health and happiness.

When your thoughts are target focused, positive and pleasant, you will find your emotions, actions and results mirror this. When you allow your thoughts to focus on problems and challenges, you will find your experience, emotions, progress and journey reflect this negativity.

Govern your thoughts to the same degree as you govern your actions and you will learn to appreciate that the world around you is highly malleable. Be they positive or negative, thoughts become things. The choice is yours.

Damage limitation

If you do take a wrong turn, you can reduce the amount of damage that's caused by righting your wrongs. For every crumb you drop, there is an opportunity for resolution. Initiate this as soon as possible.

The first step is to have the self-awareness to identify and acknowledge where and when you have created negative energy. Instead of becoming defensive and apportioning blame, you need to review and reflect on the situation. Carve out dedicated time and headspace to understand what has taken place and explore the cause and effect of the experience or event. Park your ego. Observe your emotions, but don't absorb them. Instead, reflect on them pragmatically in a bid to consider all perspectives.

When things go wrong, it can be difficult to make them better, but exceptionally easy to make them worse. To limit any lasting damage and ensure you leave no negative energy behind, the next objective is to aim for a resolution.

No one enjoys difficult conversations. They can present anxiety, fear or anger for all involved, so most people would rather not have them, but approaching a challenging conversation well will always have a positive outcome.

An effective way to neutralise any negative energy and limit further damage from mistakes you make is to approach the conversation with the mindset that you are wrong. Communicate this mindset to the other parties involved and you will disarm the negative energy, avoid emotions taking over and allow a productive conversation to take place to explore a potential resolution or bring closure for all sides. In the short term, these are hard conversations to have, but by doing the right thing, picking up your crumbs and limiting the damage, you will be preserving your Karma Credits and investing in the long-term wellbeing of all involved.

Take pride in apology

Taking pride in apology is one of the most underutilised ways to resolve issues, clear crumbs and generate Karma Credits. Within a society of increasingly sensitive and ego-driven mindsets, many of us have fallen into the trap of taking everything personally. The fight to be right has become more important than stepping up and admitting when we are wrong.

When the majority make a mistake or find themselves in the wrong, their default response, subconsciously or otherwise, is to become defensive. They fight to the death and hope ego, energy or emotion can get them through it. Crumbs are dropped, negative energy is produced and Karma Credits are lost. This is a lose-lose scenario.

If you observe the masses and do the opposite – acknowledge your mistakes and take pride in your apology – you will quickly realise that everyone leaves happy, and your trail of crumbs diminishes. At the earliest opportunity, instead of getting defensive and letting your ego take over, offer a genuine and heartfelt apology and see what reaction this elicits.

When you can take as much pride in being wrong as you do in being right, the positive energy you experience and the respect you gain will increase to a level you likely don't know exists. This is a win-win scenario. If you need to say sorry, then say it whenever you can as it will neutralise a negative situation. The alternative is to get your back up and get defensive, and there's no value in that. Everyone involved in the conversation leaves feeling upset.

When you make a mistake, turn a negative into a positive and take pride in your apology. I cannot encourage you enough to own your apology.

MAKE AMENDS

Over the years, I have spent time reflecting on my actions, what crumbs I have left behind and how best to go about resolving them. Here, I will share a couple of examples with you.

After a conversation with one of my team members, I realised that I'd given them the wrong instructions and it had cost this person a lot of time. Instead of sending a message or email, I picked up the phone and explained that I was concerned. I acknowledged that we'd agreed a course of action to take, but I was completely wrong, and I apologised for wasting a lot of their valuable time.

Immediately, any potential negative energy was neutralised. They responded by saying they completely understood and that we all make mistakes. It was then no issue at all.

In a joint-venture business deal, most of the money had been divided up between all parties as we went along, but a small amount remained with me. Everyone involved knew this needed to be calculated and distributed, but weeks turned into months, months turned into years, and I carried this crumb and the unconscious tension it caused around with me.

One day, the pressure surfaced. I knew I had to deal with it and get the final balance payment to my business partners, and it needed to happen before they came to me. I was already on borrowed time; it wasn't right that they should have to chase me for something that was my obligation. I needed to own this, and I did. Crumb cleared, all parties happy and the balance of karma restored.

SIX

Your Life

Life /laɪf/ Noun: The period between birth and
death, or the experience or state of being alive[13]

Having provided various insights and
directions throughout this book, I will
now introduce you to several actions and
mindsets that you can put in practice today to
generate Karma Credits. These will help you
to instil Karma Credits into your daily routine
to improve future experiences, relationships

and your life in general. There is a great quote from Oscar Wilde that emphasises the difference between those who invest in generating Karma Credits and those who do not: 'To live is the rarest thing in the world. Most people exist, that is all.'[14]

I don't think anyone can explain exactly how karma works. What I do know is that I have spent a decade refining and implementing the practice of Karma Credits and today, I am someone I can be proud of. I enjoy my life, I am positive even when faced with challenges and I can honestly say that I feel secure, comfortable and ridiculously content as a result. Now I want the same for you.

If you want to observe how the masses behave and do the opposite, I can assure you that integrating the daily practice of Karma Credits into your life will achieve this. As a result, you will transform the quality of your experiences today, tomorrow and beyond. Just remember that success and failure are both predictable.

Cha-ching versus uh-ugh

At the highest level, generating Karma Credits is about making the shift from prioritising your own needs, wants and desires to a primary focus on the needs, wants and requirements of others. Although society has driven many cultures into a place of fierce competition, cap-italism or violence, the idea here is to move away from a life and mindset of fear to one of love. Make it your daily purpose to serve and add value to those you meet.

To help anchor this ethos, here is a game you can play. When you complete an act of service or a RAK, make a 'cha-ching' noise, either in your head or out loud. Acknowledge that you have just generated Karma Credits and it's win-win.

When you make a mistake, lose your temper or are rude to someone, you need to pay the price to balance the books. Make an 'uh-ugh' noise, either in your head or out loud, to recognise that your balance is reduced.

The aim of this daily game is to generate more Karma Credits than you lose. If you want to supercharge the accountability and extended value of this game, share it with your family and friends. By using these sound effects collectively to acknowledge the actions you all take, you will hold each other accountable and inspire and motivate accordingly. When you get more 'cha-chings' than 'uh-ughs', you will see how success and failure are both predictable.

It is unlikely that Karma Credits will have you cashing in the winning lottery ticket anytime soon, but once you have generated and sustained a positive balance, much like an insurance policy, they will step in and get you across the line in a critical moment of need. I have experienced a life of struggle and scarcity, but also one of enjoyment and abundance, and I fully believe Karma Credits are the insurance policy that protects me and acts as a safety net when I need to call on it.

This could be anything from avoiding a serious injury when tripping over something to taking on and succeeding with an extremely high-risk business deal or achieving against all odds a target I have set for myself. As long as I have given maximum effort to maintaining a high balance of Karma Credits, I often find myself on the other side of a close call, a near miss or a record-breaking victory asking, 'How on earth did that happen?'

My efforts in developing this process have been solely focused on increasing the positive. How can I generate Karma Credits to add more value, enjoyment and positivity to my life and to those around me, even when challenges present themselves and times are hard?

It is necessary to acknowledge that you reap what you sow, and Karma Credits are no different. Your cha-chings and uh-ughs show that Karma Credits can work positively and negatively. If you continue to wrong your neighbour, treat people poorly or be rude or selfish, you can expect without doubt this negative energy to return to you.

Invest every day in generating and maintaining a positive Karma Credits balance. This is your insurance policy and safety net through both the good times and the bad. Give and you shall receive.

The compound effect

In his book *The Compound Effect*,[15] keynote speaker and author Darren Hardy describes this term as meaning the way in which we can gain huge rewards from small actions that may even seem insignificant. Over time, though, they accumulate into something far greater than we could ever imagine. So it is with the practice of generating Karma Credits.

Initially, the practice of generating Karma Credits may feel awkward and uncomfortable. As psychologist and author Susan Jeffers advises in her excellent book on taking control of your life, you need to *Feel the Fear and Do It Anyway.*[16]

An easy start is to recognise the efforts and service of those you know around you. Slow down and enjoy a couple of 'one-minute moments' where you show them your gratitude. These are quick wins; they add value to others, and you will enjoy your experience of connecting on a higher level. The joy that you feel from your first cha-ching, generating your first Karma Credits, will prove to you this works and grow your confidence in developing it further.

To build on this, try something more outward-facing – let people out in traffic or ask a cashier in the supermarket how their day is going. As your confidence and momentum build, move on to saying hello to everyone you pass and performing RAKs for strangers.

At the same time, acknowledge the occasions when you don't let a driver out or you walk past someone on your street and don't say hello. Anchor it with an audible 'uh-ugh' to recognise those missed opportunities to generate Karma Credits. Before long, you will develop an internal sense of obligation.

With an increased level of self-awareness, you will observe how good it feels to generate Karma Credits and how bad it feels when you miss an opportunity. Your initial awkwardness and discomfort will give way to an addiction – a positive one. Your actions and their results will accumulate and your practice of generating Karma Credits will develop still further.

The world around you is completely malleable. As you accumulate your Karma Credits, you'll find your heart opens, your smile stretches wide and those around you seem more welcoming and genuinely pleased to see you.

Do the right thing

As you proactively put these actions into practice, you will create positive energy and generate Karma Credits, but it may seem less obvious how you apply this reactively into your day-to-day mindset, mantras, emotions, attitudes and responses. In today's world, the masses seem to be driven by egos and motivations to gain, accompanied by an attitude to win at all costs. To adjust this mindset, you must strip back to basics and rewire your brain. Doing the right thing is one of the most important attributes of generating Karma Credits.

When you are confronted with conflict, disagreement or angry disputes, consciously park the ego, observe the emotion rather than absorb it, and bite your tongue. Engage your brain and ask yourself, 'What is the right thing to do here?'

Sometimes the answer will involve acknowledging that you are wrong. Other times, it may involve putting your hand in your pocket and absorbing a financial loss or incurring a cost. Either way, take pride in doing the right thing. Seek only to establish what the right thing to do is and proceed with doing just that.

With a shift in focus from winning transactions to doing the right thing, you can trade a short-term gain for developing positive relationships and playing the long game. I have decades of experience in both and one of the most significant lessons I have learned with

Karma Credits is to favour relationships over transactions. It is also one of the most challenging to establish when you seemingly gain less today for an elusive tomorrow that may or may not yield a return.

When you give or lose something in a transaction today in the interest of doing the right thing for a potential return from the relationship sometime in the future, you enhance your trajectory of growth, the quality of your reputation and the general positivity of your energy. You then generate your Karma Credits and create your safety net.

Tune into those around you and notice who is out for all they can get. Who is only thinking about themselves? Who has a short-sighted mindset? Consider how much enjoyment they experience. How rewarded are they in the medium to long term? How much growth or development do they achieve?

Now compare them to people you know who are generous. Those who sometimes take a hit, but always do the right thing. They give more than they take and generally have a selfless attitude and long-term relationship-based view on how they go about their business. What do you notice about their energy, relationships and trajectory?

Life, love, business, friendship, growth and success are all long games. There is no end destination; you need to practise the generation of Karma Credits daily. After two decades of experiencing both success and failure, I have now grasped this concept and it is instilled in who I am and everything I do.

PLAY THE LONG GAME

In 2015 I worked on a seven-figure project with a new joint venture partner which went six figures over budget and took a year longer to deliver than intended. While this was unfortunate, it is not uncommon. However, rather than sharing the impact of this with my partner, I instead decided to absorb the losses myself, which meant I did not see any profit while my investor achieved the full returns they had expected.

Had I focused solely on the transaction here, it is unlikely we would have worked together again. However, by putting my hand in my pocket, prioritising the relationship and focusing on the long game, the outcome was that we continued to work together, doing bigger and bigger deals. Over the following decade, we went on to form a long-standing partnership, which has been highly lucrative. This would have been highly unlikely had I taken my chips off the table when we first worked together.

Playing the long game is one of the most advanced ways that you can introduce the generation of Karma Credits into your life. Relationships over transactions is the key to taking it to the ultimate level.

I take so many hits on a daily basis. I could be 30%, 40%, even 50% more wealthy today in monetary terms if I took every opportunity, but instead, I'm constantly giving and making win-win compromises. I'm playing the long game.

The reality is, while my growth might be slower than some people's, it's consistent and it's secure. When I look back at the decisions where I paid a cost but did the right thing, I realise how well they have served me today. I am proof that doing the right thing can positively affect your life.

I look at my life today and feel grateful for where I am. I'm adding value to other people. I've made some bad decisions in the past and I've had some horrendous personal and professional experiences, but I've owned those mistakes, learned from them and ultimately been well rewarded for my actions.

While I don't tend to focus on what other people think, I believe we all do to a certain extent. There will always be exceptions, but in the main, I do think I am perceived as a good person and that's important to me. I want to be a good person. I want to be seen to be a good person. That makes me feel good.

YOUR LIFE

When I look back at my life, I want to be secure in the knowledge that I gave more than I took. I added value to those on my journey. I encourage you to do the same.

Play the long game. It's all a long game.

Conclusion

There is a lot to digest in this book, so in conclusion, I will summarise the key points. These will set you up for a full, positive life. By embracing the universal law of Karma Credits, you can enjoy wealth, health and happiness.

It is important you practise the generation of Karma Credits anonymously. This is not an opportunity to beat your chest. I'm sharing my experience with you as I have a privileged opportunity to do so; I haven't done the things

I've described in this book to post about them on social media. I encourage you to observe anonymity too.

You need to move from a competitive, ego-driven one-on-one mindset to that of a connected oneness where we are all part of the same journey. Transition from a mindset of fear and scarcity to one of love and abundance and you will quickly see your life and the world around you change for the better.

You can live in a big house, but you are buried in a small coffin. The wealth in your life is defined not by what you gain and what you take, but by who you are, what you give and how you feel. Giving is living.

Have a look in the mirror every day and ask, 'Am I proud of myself? Am I behaving in a way that I'm proud of? Am I doing things that are congruent with me being who I want to be?' If you're having a bad run, burning yourself out, succumbing to low discipline and bad habits,

CONCLUSION

behaving poorly to your friends, colleagues or
family, say, 'No, this is not me', then get back
to the basics and sort it out. Every action has a
consequence.

Slow and steady wins the race so start small
today. Give more than you take and focus on
adding value at every opportunity rather than
taking it. With positive thoughts, actions and
energy, you will generate more Karma Credits
than you lose. These will protect you in both
the good times and the bad.

I have explored both ends of the spectrum over
the last twenty years and have found the blueprint that enables me to generate and maintain
my positive Karma Credits balance. This blueprint has served me well and defined my life.
Now I feel good, confident in who I am and
what I do. I have a safety net and insurance
policy for when I need it.

My blueprint is now yours to practise and take
forward. Seize the day, act now and get out

97

there. 'Cha-ching' yourself to your first Karma Credits and discover that success and failure are both predictable.

I wish you the best of luck.

References

1   Karma Credits is a trademark
2   'Karma', dictionary.com (no date), www.
    dictionary.com/browse/karma, accessed
    July 2022
3   Venerable Mahasi Sayadaw, 'The theory
    of karma in Buddhism' (Buddhanet,
    2004) www.buddhanet.net/e-learning/
    karma.htm, accessed June 2022
4   'noble', lexico.com (no date), www.
    lexico.com/definition/noble, accessed
    July 2022

5 'experience', lexico.com (no date), www. lexico.com/definition/experience, accessed July 2022

6 P Mateos-Aparicio and A Rodríguez-Moreno, 'The impact of studying brain plasticity', *Frontiers in Cellular Neuroscience* (2019) www.frontiersin.org/articles/10.3389/fncel.2019.00066/full

7 'recognize', dictionary.cambridge.org (no date), https://dictionary.cambridge.org/dictionary/english/recognize, accessed July 2022

8 J Rohn (@OfficialJimRohn), 'One of the greatest gifts…' (Tweet, 26 October 2017), https://twitter.com/officialjimrohn/status/923542404820500480, accessed June 2022

9 'What is the law of reciprocity?' (Elevate, no date), https://elevatepromo.com/what-is-the-law-of-reciprocity, accessed July 2022

10 'guilt', dictionary.com (no date), www. dictionary.com/browse/guilt, accessed July 2022

REFERENCES

11 B Proctor, 'Everything that's coming into your life…' (Facebook post, 21 April 2013), www.facebook.com/OfficialBobProctor/posts/everything-that-is-coming-into-your-life-you-are-attracting-into-your-life-and-i/10151560348949421, accessed June 2022

12 R Byrne, *The Secret* (Atria Books, 2006)

13 'life', dictionary.cambridge.org (no date), https://dictionary.cambridge.org/dictionary/english/life, accessed July 2022

14 O Wilde, *The Soul of Man under Socialism* (1891)

15 D Hardy, *The Compound Effect: Jumpstart your income, your life, your success* (Hachette, 2020)

16 S Jeffers, *Feel The Fear And Do It Anyway: How to turn your fear and indecision into confidence and action* (Vermilion, 2007)

Acknowledgements

The creation of Karma Credits would not be possible without the input and impact of those around me, and the positive and challenging experiences I have had on my journey, for all of which, I am truly grateful.

The publication of this practice would not have been possible without the consistent efforts and accountability of Emma Trew, who guided and supported me in the writing of this book, and the expertise of Kathleen Steeden and the team at Rethink Press for bringing it to life.

The Author

Daniel Hill is a UK-based market-leading and award-winning serial entrepreneur. Having dedicated his adult life to the study and practice of high performance and achieved success that resulted in his retirement at the age of thirty-five, he discovered the highest-value secret in one of the most surprising places.

While Daniel's success can be widely accredited to endless study, hard graft and taking risks, a decade into this journey, he found his focus on energy and spirituality holding more weight than that on economics and strategy. With some realisations and quick wins under his belt, Daniel turned his hand to studying the mantras, mindsets and actions of various ancient texts and spiritual practices. Although he found them uncomfortable and awkward to put into practice initially, Daniel experienced the value they delivered and quickly became addicted.

Consolidating these various practices, Daniel learned how to generate positive Karma Credits in his life and created the ENERGY blueprint he shares in this book. He refers to the consistent practice of generating Karma Credits through the ups and downs of life as his insurance policy and the secret to his success.

THE AUTHOR

- www.property-entrepreneur.co.uk
- www.facebook.com/ PropertyEntrepreneurOfficial
- www.facebook.com/groups/ PropertyEntrepreneur
- www.linkedin.com/in/danielhillptg
- www.linkedin.com/company/ propertyentrepreneur
- @propertyentrepreneur_
- www.youtube.com/channel/ UC8Ex7TwF5BH_xxSwZ9VnGmg
- @property_entrepreneur
- https://podcasts.apple.com/ gb/podcast/the-official- property-entrepreneur-podcast/ id1498618503